Saltwater Fish and Reef Tanks

From Beginner to Expert

By: Zechariah Blanchard

This book is dedicated to all the amazing people out there that share my passion for discovery and learning. Reef tanks are an amazing way to further your love of science and nature.

I also want to thank my wife, fellow hobbyists, and close friends for pushing me to finish this book.

Table of Contents

Preface

Growing up, I often heard how hard it was to maintain a saltwater aquarium. Still, my father and many others managed to have successful tanks. Eventually, this led to me getting my own. I had quite the learning experience with my first reef tank. A lot of it came the hard way, but it gave me the knowledge and experience to help people keep from making the same mistakes.

Quite a few years later I decided to open a store and went through the licensing, paperwork, acquiring the equipment, and finding a location. A lot of people I had been helping with their tank at the time came to build out the store with me. It was not much to look at, but it was a start. I taught classes there on many different aspects of reef-keeping. It helped me harness what a new hobbyist needs to know.

We grew the store over time and built a name for great customer service. Customers would travel to our store from as far as several hours away to speak to me about their tanks.

During some of these discussions the idea of writing a book came up and I decided to write Saltwater Fish and Reef Tanks. I had written a book in 2010, why not 2012? That was several years ago, but I am proud to now release the book that came of this great adventure I had with hundreds of amazing people. I wish I still had my store to help them, but I don't. This book will serve as a great substitute that has far wider reach.

I want to help people get into this hobby and enjoy their tank. We should all know it isn't as hard as people think to keep a saltwater fish or reef tank. If you are new to saltwater aquariums (first few years), sit back, relax, and enjoy, I wrote this book just for you.

Introduction

Nearly two years before I opened my bricks and mortar aquarium store, I had a horrible crash in a 125 gallon tank being used to house a lot of expensive coral. I must have lost thousands of dollars during the crash. That's something I will never forget. It seemed like an eternity; watching all my hard work and money slowly die.

First, I noticed the SPS (Small Polyp Stony Coral) turning brown. Then, my LPS (Large Polyp Stony Coral) started to recede. I immediately prepped for a water change. Being in the hobby for many years I knew the only way to stop a water quality crash (or slow it down) was a large water change. I mixed fifty-five gallons of fresh saltwater and performed a large water change. Things did not improve; they got worse. I performed another large water change, added carbon, and began frantically testing my water.

Water testing didn't show anything out of the ordinary. I tested again but nothing changed. I performed yet another large water change with no difference in the results. After checking the online forums and calling several local stores, I decided it was out of my league, so I went to get my water tested. The first store told me everything checked out. The second store said the same. With the same information I was stumped. I kept working on the problem. I couldn't believe it when I realized it.

The hydrometer for my tank had been soaking in saltwater for a while and the float in it absorbed minerals. This caused a lower salinity reading than was actually in the water. Because of this small error I was mixing very salty water for my tank and suffocating and irritating my livestock to death. My refractometer confirmed my suspicion and I corrected the problem. The coral that was still alive recovered over the next few months.

Disasters happen in this hobby all the time. Small things become large problems fast. A book like this one would have saved me a lot of money and headache. I am about to walk you through everything from buying a tank to maintaining a thriving reef. But, you won't learn the hard way like so many of us have. You have the answers right here.

My First Saltwater Tank

Around 1998 or 1999 I decided to make the leap from freshwater to saltwater. I figured it couldn't be that hard – after all, my father had them as I was growing up. All I needed was a tank, a filter, some sand, water, and light so that I could see everything. It sounds easy enough, so I got started.

I found a 55 gallon tank at a garage sale down the street. It came with gravel, a hood with light, pumps, and two filters. I hit the jackpot for like 15 bucks (More then, but still a small cost). I took the tank home and elicited my brothers` help in setting it up. We decided to make a trip to the store before starting. Off we went to the only store in the entire city that sold saltwater.

When we got there, we decided to go back and take a look at the fish, coral, and invertebrates. At the time we just called it "live stuff." There were corals, crabs, starfish, shrimp, and fish. Little did we know what they really were. We felt like such newbs asking questions. The salt was expensive. I remember thinking, "Man, I can get it at the grocery store for cheaper than that! How can anyone charge that much for sand and salt?"

We came to the same conclusion we should get everything from the beach and made a trip to the hardware store to get buckets. The beach came immediately after. Upon arrival we grabbed enough water and sand for a 55 gallon tank. The climb back to the car seemed like a PT session with a seasoned Drill Instructor. Those buckets sure got heavy.

We got home and put the sand in first. Then we grabbed some rocks from the front yard and put them in the tank. I had no idea what live rock was, but rock looked natural in a saltwater tank. So, we poured the water in and started the two hang on back filters. Extremely pleased with ourselves, we sat down and watched the tank for a while. We decided to go the following day and get some coral, fish, and inverts.

The following morning we went to the beach and got hermit crabs and snails. The inlet was littered with them. We must have grabbed a few hundred of each. One the way home we stopped at the aquarium store and decided to get some fish and coral. "Woah! A saltwater fish costs how much? Okay, well, we want the yellow fish, the orange and black one, and that rock that's moving."

Turns out, we got a yellow tang, a clownfish, and some star polyps. We paid what seemed like an enormous sum of money and made the trip back home. We dumped the hermits and snails in the tank. We didn't think we were new to acclimation, so we floated the bags in the water for about 5 minutes, and then opened them to let a little water in, and a little more, and then dumped the fish and corals in – store water and all.

The star polyps didn't come out all the way like they had at the store, so we got a few jet pumps and threw them in on the sides. They created some flow and the fish seemed to like it, too. It was not long before I started telling people to come and see the tank. It was amazing; two fish, one coral, and hundreds of hermits and snails!

Then we spent quite some time working on the rock structure. Eventually, it looked like ancient ruins or something. Blocks stacked unnaturally on top of each other.

Over time we began to notice the star polyps not looking too great, so we put them as high as we could get them. We heard from someone at the store that they like a lot of light, and we were waiting on a new light we ordered. If I recall correctly, they were PC lights. Man, 350 bucks for a little PC light seemed like a lot of money. The tank was going to be great.

Before the light arrived we had a death. The yellow tang died and was being eaten by hermits. We went back to the saltwater store and talked to them about it. They told us that it happens sometimes and we should try again. They had a few random fish, and some small coral pieces. We grabbed two cheap fish the guy called damsels and a few of what the guy called mushrooms. When we got home we did the same thing for acclimation.

A few days later the clownfish and some snails died. The hermits were having a field day eating whatever passed on. We thought we were just having bad luck with fish. This was getting expensive. We went back to the aquarium store and told the guy what happened. He told us the tank was probably cycling.

What the heck is cycling?!? My tank might be killing my fish!? I just set this thing up, I told him. We got the sand from the beach, the water from the ocean, some old rock, and set it up. Feeling kind of stupid at this point, I asked him what cycling means.

Well, it is a break in period for the bacteria in your tank. Without going through a cycle the tank can't handle the waste created by the livestock. Waste leaves a lot of ammonia and other toxins in the water – and the toxins stress out and kill your livestock. It usually takes about 6 weeks for this to end.

That was a lot to grasp. I thought we were done. Now we have to wait six weeks! It is like an eternity... At least this will give us time to think about what we want in the aquarium. And the tank sat for 6 weeks with two damsels, a star polyp rock, and some hermit crabs lunching on snails that were dying.

After the tank finished cycling, we went to the fish store. We had been saving our money and were ready to buy some cool stuff. The store had like 8 corals in stock! We hit the coral lotto.

We picked up about 3 new pieces of coral, two yellow tangs, two clownfish, a sand sifting star (to clean the brown off the sand), and a feather duster. We also got a heater. They had a few different kinds, but the cheaper one seemed to be the right way to go.

When we got home we installed the heater and acclimated the fish, coral, and starfish. It was so beautiful now! Look at those corals. Under the new power compact light everything looked great - except the star polyp. It was still kind of irritated from the cycling and lack of light.

No matter, we still stared at that tank for hours watching the amazing life swim around this environment we created. Before we went to bed we took one last look and turned the light off.

We got up in the morning and went right to the tank. All the fish were floating except one. One of the clownfish was alive, but he didn't look good. We touched the tank and it was hot. The heater wasn't working properly.

We removed the heater and began pouring cold water into the tank from the tap. It needed to be topped off anyway. Then, we did a five gallon water change to add more cold water.

After hours of work, we got all the dead stuff out and brought the temperature down to about 78 degrees. We had lost so much. It was a rough beginning. Still, we persevered and made another trip all the way in town to exchange the heater.

The store offered to replace it with the same model, but we decided to spend a few extra dollars to avoid killing more livestock.

It took several months for us to get past the first few hurdles. There were outbreaks of ich, parasites, fighting, water problems, and more. We knew so little back then. That has changed.

There may have been a lot of mistakes, and I made many more, but I learned a lot along the way. I remember what it is like to be back at the beginning.

In the early stages of the hobby there are more questions than answers. There is so much to learn it seems daunting. It really isn't that hard.

We often hear naysayers with the same experience as I had saying, "That hobby is very expensive and impossible. After you spend a ton of money and time, everything will just die. There is no way to do it. Just put your money in a better place. Give it to me if you just want to waste it. I won't even charge you for saving your time."

These are the naysayers of our great hobby. There are corals in captivity that no longer exist in the wild. We have life that lives only inside a hobbyist reef. These passionate hobbyists do whatever they can to promote the health of these endangered species. It is sort of like an ark of coral.

Through this book I am going to help you learn everything you need to know about the hobby. I will do my best to make it easy for you. Follow along this book, or just use it as a reference. No matter, it is going to be one of the best investments you have ever made in this hobby.

Before the Decision to Buy

There are some things you should know before making the decision to purchase a saltwater aquarium. Actually, there are a lot of things you should know before buying a tank. Things are changing in this hobby daily, but the basics remain the same. We will focus on these basics.

The saltwater hobby is extremely fulfilling, but it's also extremely addicting. Patience is going to be your best friend – if you don't have patience then save your money and find another hobby.

There are as many opinions out there as there are hobbyists, but most opinions come from hobbyists with less than a year of experience. Actually, the majority of hobbyists have less than a year of experience.

The first thing I tell most people about this hobby is how easy the hobby can be. If you can follow a few simple steps, you can own a beautiful saltwater aquarium – be it reef or fish only.

Every saltwater tank requires three things to be healthy and grow: water quality, water flow, and lighting. If you can create these environmental requirements, you can own a saltwater tank. (We will speak in depth about these soon).

After getting past the basics, I let everyone know this hobby is as addicting as it is rewarding. I have never found another hobby which has given back to me as much as I have put into it – as far as feelings of personal accomplishment and reward.

You get from this hobby what you – or someone else by proxy – put into it. I never seem to be finished with my tanks. (In all fairness, most people think my tanks great, but I continue my quest for perfection).

Patience is probably the single most important thing after water quality, flow, and lighting. This hobby does not start out fast and can very easily turn for the worst. Take your time.

Dumping money into a saltwater aquarium before you know what is going on inside the glass walls is very dangerous financially and for the livestock. It takes time to build a happy reef. We will discuss the aquarium cycle details in proceeding sections.

Recent research has shown what long time hobbyists have known for years – most hobbyist get out of the hobby within the first year due to complications. These complications are more due to a lack of education and understanding than they are due to actual complications in the saltwater hobby.

The biggest problem with this is they tend to be the naysayers scaring potential hobbyists away. Their opinions are often negative, poorly researched, and wrong. Be careful who you listen to.

Every potential or current hobbyist should know about tank size and livestock availability. There are a lot of choices when it comes to saltwater fish, coral, and invertebrates. Many have special needs.

Compatibility with tank size is one of the most important things to consider when buying your first tank. You don't want to get an aquarium and set it up, only to find out you can't add the livestock you want.

These things in no way tell you about everything you should know, but they are a good representation of the things you should consider before making the decision to get into the hobby. Most people won't figure these things out until they are already a thousand or more dollars into the hobby. Considering these things along with the proceeding sections before you decide to buy will save you considerable amounts of money.

Deciding on Tank Size

There are many things to consider when making the decision on aquarium size. You will want to think about the livestock going into the aquarium, the space allotted for the tank, the budget, and the maintenance constraints.

Because each one of these is important to your overall success rate, we will talk about them individually. By the end of this section you should feel comfortable making a decision on aquarium size.

One of the most important decisions when contemplating aquarium size is the livestock you plan to keep. Coral tends to do poor in deep tanks because artificial light has a hard time penetrating deeper than 24 inches. This of course depends on the exact type of light used, but it's a good rule of thumb.

Certain types of fish require a large tank to stay healthy. Tangs for instance require 75 or more gallons of water. This is a minimum for most tangs to stay happy and healthy. On the reverse end, some fish get lost in large tanks and prefer smaller ones. Clown gobies for instance are so small they can get lost in the system of a large tank.

Basically, open ocean fish need a lot of room to roam. Small fish, which, primarily stay in the reef rocks and move very little, can usually do well in small tanks. Either way, considering the type of livestock you are planning on having in your aquarium before you purchase is a smart move. Look the livestock up to ensure you make the right decision.

The second thing you might want to consider when purchasing your aquarium is the available space. If the tank is going into a small bedroom it might be good to start small. Likewise, if you live on a floor higher than the first, you may want to consider what it would involve to move a large aquarium up to your place. Also consider how safe the tank would be on the floor of your home.

Large aquariums make great showpieces in the middle of a family or living room. They can also make great pieces in a large bedroom. I love large tanks. But, before you sink your hard earned money into a large system, make sure you check on the available space.

It might even be a good idea to place some tape or cardboard on the floor - for a week or two - where you are considering placing tank. This will give you a temporary understanding of where the reef will be located.

Moving a large tank more than once is quite a hassle. Not only can it disrupt the cycle, it can take hours or days depending on your experience level and speed.

This brings us to the budget question. Some people think the main cost is the tank and stand. I am here to tell you this is only a fraction of the overall cost. Small tanks can start at a few hundred and go up to thousands.

I have a customer who has spent nearly six thousand dollars on a 75 gallon reef tank and he isn't finished. (Mind you it is the most high tech 75 gallon I have ever seen).

The largest aquariums cost up into the millions and are custom made on location. These tank builds are often found on national television shows. Some of them need full time employees to keep them maintained.

Purchasing the tank and stand used can help save considerable money. Usually, this can be done on a website like craigslist or a local saltwater forum. You will still need to account for costs like sand, rock, water, pumps, lighting, and filtration. All of which comes before livestock.

Saltwater aquariums need a good quality live sand to maintain a healthy cycle. I recommend live aragonite sand because it will help maintain the water parameters.

Don't use imitation or synthetic sands and steer clear of crushed coral – they cause problems. Your sand should be thick grain for reef tanks. This will keep it from blowing around. Fine sands are best for bottom feeders like stingrays.

Live sand will cost you between one and three dollars a pound. You are going to need about one pound per gallon.

The rock used in saltwater aquariums is live rock. Live rock is covered in bacteria and other life which maintain the water quality in your tank. Live rock is probably going to be one of the single most expensive things you purchase for this hobby.

Quality live rock can cost from four to around eight dollars a pound. Some rare live rock can cost as much as twenty or more dollars a pound.

You are going to need between a pound and a pound and a half per gallon. This adds up fast. Some people choose to purchase their live rock in small amounts over the course of several months. It helps to spread the cost.

The trick to buying good live rock is considering the shape or texture and weight or porosity. Good live rock is not extremely heavy and has good shape for stacking.

When purchasing rock it is important to know the difference between base rock, cycled rock, live rock, and *quality* live rock. Base rock is simply clean rock ready to go into your aquarium. Base rock is usually dry and contains no bacteria.

Cycled rock comes in different forms: cured and uncured. Uncured rock comes with dead organics on it and can help hard cycle your tank. Cycled live rock doesn't have dead organics and is ready to go into a cycled tank. Uncured rock is okay for new tanks, but bad for cycled tanks. Cured rock is good for both. It takes three to eight weeks to cure live rock.

Live rock also comes in two basic types. There is a basic live rock and a quality live rock. Basic live rock is usually heavy and lacks good shape. This rock is okay, but it is usually in your best interest to spend just a little more on quality live rock. Quality live rock is lighter by volume and has a lot more holes for bacteria and pods to grow. It usually costs a little more by the pound, but you get more in volume and filtration out of quality live rock.

Most saltwater stores sell saltwater ready to go into your tank. Usually this has a cost of about a dollar a gallon, but can range depending on location. Local stores will usually rent out water jugs for a deposit. This allows you to purchase enough water for your tank all at once. Some stores will deliver water to you.

Maintaining healthy coral requires a lot of water movement. Most reef tanks have several pumps aside from the pump in the sump that returns water.

These extra pumps help move the water in the aquarium at a rate of 20 to 30 times an hour. Meaning 20 to 30 times the total volume moves through a pump every hour. If your return pump pushes ten times tank volume, you will need one to two additional pumps at a rate of ten times tank volume.

Getting a quality pump is going to play a crucial role - not only in the longevity of the pump, but - in the amount of heat it generates in the aquarium. Saltwater aquariums need to maintain very specific parameters. Temperature is one of the most important.

Pumps usually run between fifty and several hundred dollars. Large ones can cost into the thousands.

Lighting is a big deal on a reef tank. If you plan to setup a fish only system, you can get just about any lighting you want, but should consider the fish coloration under different lighting, not to mention, algae growth. In a reef tank, it is a good idea to get quality lighting to help your reef grow and look great.

When it comes to lighting, you should know about spectrum, par rating, longevity, heat generation, and power consumption. The basic lighting styles being used right now are metal halides, t-5s, and LEDs. Here is a short breakdown.

In the ocean, corals get certain spectrums of lighting and not others. Because most corals grow at a depth which gets more of the blue spectrum, it is important to mimic this blue light in the aquarium. Special bulbs in the 420-460nm spectrum produce the right light for corals. This light will help your corals grow fast and healthy.

Par rating is the total amount of light energy getting to a certain point in the aquarium. It is not perfect because it doesn't measure the different spectrums of light. Tanks can have a lot of par in the unusable spectrum and very little right spectrum.

Par rating is still a good general indicator of lighting in your aquarium. Most tanks have a few hundred par at the top and about one hundred par toward the bottom.

Longevity, heat generation, and power consumption are interrelated and depend on the specific type of lighting you chose. Halides use the most energy, create the most heat, and burn out the quickest. T-5's are generally next in line, and LEDs carry up the rear. Here is a little more information about halides, t-5s, and LEDs.

Metal halides are old, but are still preferred by some hobbyist due in part to the shimmer they create, and in part because they are proven. They generate a lot of heat, use a lot of energy, and the bulbs need replacing every six months.

Halides get expensive to replace at fifty or more dollars each. The fixtures can run from a hundred to a few thousand depending on size and brand.

T-5 lights are a high output florescent bulb. They create less heat than metal halides, use less energy, and put out just about as much light. It is easier to go full spectrum with t-5s because most aquariums require four or more bulbs. The problem with this is they also must be replaced every six months. This gets costly at thirty bucks a bulb. The fixtures run from fifty to a few thousand dollars depending on size and brand.

LEDs have recently gotten very popular in reef keeping. Old and new hobbyists are using LEDs over their display tanks with great success. My store used nothing but LEDs. Something to consider for now (LEDs are changing rapidly) is that LEDs do not penetrate like halides.

LEDs tend were costly in the beginning for a long time, but have come down in price considerably in recent years. The benefit is low heat production, low energy usage, and no bulb replacement for three years or 10,000 hours.

Some fixtures need to be completely replaced after three years and some have pucks you can replace. Be careful to get the right spectrum bulbs when you buy LEDS, and make sure the bulbs are quality and at least 3 watts each.

I like a mix of blue and white with a few infrared and ultraviolet LEDs thrown in the white mix. With a separate dimmer on the blue and white you can adjust the spectrum easily. Lights like this can now be found for as little as $150.00. Only use 3 watt or better LEDs.

While smaller tanks sometimes come with built in filtration, the majority of large tanks require you to install your own. There are a number of different filtration types. The basics are: overflow of some type, sump, skimmer, and return pump. Numerous things can be added, but these are generally required.

There are basically two types of overflow for larger tanks. The first type is the built in overflow. This is usually referred to as a drilled or reef ready tank. This setup is the preference of most saltwater hobbyists.

Non-drilled tanks can be modified to work like a drilled tank. This requires the use of an overflow box to create a siphon loop to the sump. Drilled tanks are part of the main setup, but overflow boxes have to be purchased separately. They usually run between fifty and a hundred dollars.

Your overflow needs to be connected to a sump. The sump houses filtration equipment - keeping it out of sight - and provides a water reservoir to maintain the level in the display. You can think of the sump like a small tank under the big tank. Sumps should be purchased at a rating higher than advertised to ensure adequate filtration and space. Sumps run between one hundred and several thousand dollars.

Skimmers are a vital part of any saltwater aquarium. They remove proteins from the water and help keep the inhabitants healthy. Proteins like waste from the fish can quickly build up in an aquarium and need to be removed. The skimmer generally goes in the sump and needs to be rated for 25% over the tank size. Skimmers run from one hundred to a thousand dollars or more.

The return pump is how water gets back up to the aquarium after gravity feeds it down your overflow. Return pumps should push a little over ten times the volume of the tank per hour. This gives a good filtration turnover rate and will help keep the water oxygenated.

Quality should be considered because these pumps are the heart of the tank – if it quits running it could be detrimental or deadly to the tank. Return pumps cost between fifty and a thousand dollars. (It doesn't hurt to have two return pumps on larger tanks in the event one goes out or gets clogged)

This brings us to maintenance. Maintenance can take from as little as a few minutes per day and an hour per week to as much as 30 minutes a day and several hours a week. It really depends on the level of cleaning detail and the extensiveness of the filtration. They usually run hand in hand – better filtration means less cleanup time, and less filtration leaves more to clean up.

You should also consider the ongoing costs. Filter media replacement, bulb replacement, water changes, and other odds and ends materials can add up fast. The costs on large tanks can sometimes feel like having an extra child to feed. Ongoing costs can run from around a dollar per gallon, per month, to as much as several dollars a gallon per month. The actual cost will depend on the depth of your sanity.

Some people don't have the time to maintain their aquarium so they hire other people to do it. Most stores have a maintenance fee they charge to come out and maintain your aquarium. The cost varies greatly from one place to another, but can start as low as a dollar a gallon per visit, to as high as five dollars a gallon per visit. Usually it ranges around two dollars per gallon and includes everything needed to maintain the aquarium.

The last thing we will discuss about tank size is water parameter maintenance. By maintenance we are talking about the change in water parameters over time. Small aquariums tend to have rapid water parameter shifts because of the low volume of water. Due to this I never recommend anything smaller than thirty gallons for a first tank. Larger tanks shift much slower because the volume of water holds the parameters.

The most rapid shifting of all is the temperature. Temperature plays a crucial role and should be maintained within a few degrees of the set temperature. Temperature swings beyond a few degrees can cause tremendous stress on livestock and leave the water deprived of much needed oxygen.

After all is said and done it comes down to what you want. It is important to find the right aquarium size for you. Too small, and the water parameters might shift rapidly. Too large, and you might not have time to give it the proper maintenance. While making the final decision, keep the livestock, the space available, the budget, and the maintenance in mind.

(Yes/No)	Yes	No
Do I have a lot of time for maintenance?	Any Size	Smaller Tank
Is my budget limited?	Smaller Tank	Any Size
Is it a reef tank?	Any Size	Any Size
Do I have a lot of space for the aquarium?	Any Size	Smaller Tank
Any Large Fish?	Larger Tank	Any Size

To help figure out the total cost to setup your tank, use the table below. This can also be used to figure the monthly and yearly cost to maintain your aquarium.

	One Time Cost	Monthly Cost	Yearly Cost
Tank & Stand			
Lighting Fixture			
Pumps			
Sand			
Rock			
Skimmer			
Sock Replacement			
Media Replacement			
Water Change			
Bulb Replacement			
Food and other Misc			
Total:			

The Aquarium Cycle and Biological Filtration

Setting up the aquarium is very simple, but first we are going to discuss the cycle. The aquarium cycle should NOT be skipped. This is where most people lose the majority of money in this hobby and quit. Trust me when I say this section is important. I will make it as easy as possible.

The aquarium cycle is basically setting up a biological filter for the tank. Saltwater aquariums can't survive without adequate filtration. Biological filters take what is in their surroundings and purify it for use by the life in the ecosystem. Everything in the contained system is part of the biological filtration. From amoebas to human beings we are all part of the cycle of the large biological filter we call earth.

Okay, so what does this have to do with the aquarium cycle you might ask? Simply put, your aquarium needs to grow a bio-filter before it can safely sustain saltwater life. We call this filtration creation cycling. Cycling starts when we get the saltwater in the tank moving and it ends when the water parameters show no signs of poisonous substance for weeks on end. Usually this takes from four to eight weeks.

Basically we start our tank with a lot of dead organic material. This comes in on the rocks, in the sand, and sometimes even in the water. This organic material breaks down after the tank begins cycling and turns into ammonia. Ammonia is extremely poisonous to saltwater livestock and will kill anything in the tank, even at low levels.

Bacteria start growing and consuming ammonia. This bacterium turns the ammonia into nitrite. As the population of ammonia eating bacteria rises, the level of ammonia drops. It is sort of like overfeeding the population of bacteria until it grows big enough to eat all the food. Once it reaches this point there will be a lot of nitrite in the water. Nitrite is also extremely poisonous.

We begin the same bacteria growth cycle with bacteria which eats nitrite and expels nitrate. As the population grows the nitrite levels go down and the nitrate levels go up. The amount of nitrate production relates directly to the amount of nitrite consumed. Likewise, the amount of nitrite created is linked directly to the amount of ammonia consumed.

Some aquarists use damsels - a hearty and inexpensive fish - to help cycle a tank. Putting them in early can ensure a faster cycle. Because they are aggressive, damsels should be removed at the end of the cycle.

There are aquarists who like to use dead shrimp to hard cycle a tank. This method jumpstarts the ammonia part of the cycle and can speed up the rest.

The last method we will discuss here is the seed start. Seeding a tank with sand, rock, or water from an established tank is a way of giving the new tank a bacteria culture from a tank that has already established an evolved bacteria population – speeding up the cycle.

When we reach the end of the aquarium cycle our test for ammonia and nitrite will read zero, while the nitrate can read from ten to sixty or more. The tables below give an indication of the type of test results you should expect at the beginning, middle, and end of the aquarium cycle. The charts are read in parts per million (ppm). Each stage of the cycle can take between one and three weeks to complete.

Stage 1	
Ammonia	0.0 ppm
Nitrite	0.0 ppm
Nitrate	0 ppm

Get the system running and keep the water topped off. Test the water weekly and check results here.

Stage 2	
Ammonia	0.25-2.0 ppm
Nitrite	0.0-0.25 ppm
Nitrate	0 ppm

The system is starting to cycle.

Stage 3	
Ammonia	0.0 ppm
Nitrite	0.25-2.0 ppm
Nitrate	0-20 ppm

Do a 20% water change around this time.

Stage 4 – End of cycle	
Ammonia	0.0 ppm
Nitrite	0.0 ppm
Nitrate	5-60 ppm

This usually comes after four to eight weeks of cycling. The aquarium is now ready to start adding livestock a little at a time. Also, remove any damsels at this time.

Setup Checklist

☐ 1) **Decide on Aquarium Size**

> Remember, tank size depends on intended livestock, budget, space available, and time for maintenance. Making the right decision before you begin will save time, headache, and money. *Please see tank size section.*

☐ 2) **Acquire the right Components**

> Depending on the size of the tank you are setting up, your budget, and time, you will need:
>
> Skimmer, Coral or Fish Light, Return and Circulating Pumps, Tank, Stand, Sump, and Heater or Chiller to Maintain 72-78 Degrees *(Only if needed)*

☐ 3) **Setup and Cycle the Aquarium**

> Setup is different for every system. The basics are: you want the return line going to the tank, the drain line going to the filter area of the sump, a skimmer in the sump, circulating pumps inside the tank, and a light on top.
> *Cycling is up to a 10 week process. Please see setup in a previous section.*

Bringing Home Livestock

It would be almost impossible to go over all different types of livestock and their individual requirements in this book. Therefore, I recommend you find either a reliable website to check or pick up a good reference book or app. Compatibility of livestock is going to be very important for the happiness of your tank and you. We will discuss the basics of livestock husbandry and acclimation in this section.

Most fish are going to have a required tank size to be happy. The reason these fish have requirements is mostly due to how they act in the wild. Open ocean swimmers like tangs tend to require tanks that are 75 gallons or larger. Small fish, which don't move much like gobies, can do well in a small aquarium.

A good rule of thumb: open ocean fish - like tangs - need tanks 75 gallons and larger. Reef swimmers - like angels - need 40 gallons or more. Fish that perch - like gobies - or move very little can usually be happy in tanks as small as ten gallons. Each species has its own requirements, but these are good general guidelines.

Another thing you will want to consider when picking up livestock is how well it plays with others. Plays well with others will be denoted by a "Reef Safe" tag. Reef Safe livestock does well with almost anything, including shrimp, corals, clams, and other fish. It is important to note, even reef safe fish can be killers. The smart hobbyist will watch for aggressive fish no matter the safety level.

Plays well with most will be denoted by a "Caution with Reef" tag. Caution livestock will require a little more research on your part – they usually don't do well with one type of livestock. Sometimes they are in this category because they *can* nip at corals, clams, and other livestock.

And most other livestock is going to be some type of predatory life denoted by the "Not Reef Safe" tag. This livestock is predatory and hunts something - be it coral, fish, or invertebrates.

It is not fun to find out you lost all your livestock to a predatory fish or invertebrate. Don't trust your local store to tell you. Most employees at local aquarium stores do not have the experience to know or the desire to ask. They prefer to assume you already know everything about the piece you are buying. This gets a lot of people in trouble early on.

Let's assume you have done your research and picked out some great pieces of livestock to take home. Now what? Do I just dump them in? NO!

Saltwater Livestock must be acclimated properly or it is likely to die. Most people lose a lot of livestock during acclimation and think it is just a part of the cost of the hobby. It is not part of the cost. Lack of education is what costs most people money.

It is important to point out that you **NEVER** want to mix store water – or any other water – with your tank water. Store water can contain copper, contaminants, and or parasites. Mixing any water with your water can give you problems and should be avoided.

A lot of books and guides show you how to acclimate by mixing water in the bag inside the tank. Always acclimate outside the tank and never introduce water from another tank into your eco-system.

See the following chapter for an in depth guide to acclimation. Make a copy of it and stick it under your tank. Following a good guide can save as many as 4 out of 5 fish.

Acclimating Livestock

Acclimation is one of the most dangerous times for your livestock. The water parameters of the ocean rarely ever change. Even when they do, it is extremely slow.

If you do not acclimate properly and the water parameters change too rapidly, it is likely your livestock will go into shock and may even die.

Acclimation is also a good time for the current aquarium inhabitants to get acquainted to the new addition. Done properly this can drastically reduce the chances of your old and new livestock fighting.

Another reason that acclimation is important is because stress can leave your livestock susceptible to sickness like ich. Stress from improper acclimation and shipment breaks down the slim coating on your livestock. This slim coat is very important in the protection against disease, fungus, ich, and bacterial infections.

See chapter on Marine Ich for more information.

In short, your livestock is more likely to get sick and or die if it is not properly acclimated. The short time it takes to properly acclimate your livestock is far worth the protection it awards your investment.

Fish Acclimation

1. Turn the lights off – in order to avoid cooking your new fish - and let the bag float in the tank for 15 minutes.

2. Open the bag and place the fish into a container with the bag water – ensuring the fish stays covered with bag-water.

   It is always a good idea to add an air stone to the container. This keeps the oxygen and pH levels high, and circulates the water in the container to lower stress and smooth acclimation.

3. Over the course of 30 minutes add a little water from the aquarium every 5 minutes in order to acclimate the fish to your aquarium parameters.

   Steady/slow drip line from the tank works best.

4. Remove the fish from the acclimation water and dip the fish in a separate container of water from the aquarium before placing the fish into your tank.

5. Keep the lights in the aquarium off for at least one hour to allow the new inhabitant to acclimate to the surroundings.

6. Discard wastewater and clean up area.

7. Watch your new and old livestock for compatibility issues – close for about ten minutes and every hour or so for the rest of the day.

    This should give you ample indication if they are not compatible.

Acclimating Invertebrates

1. Turn the lights off – in order to avoid cooking your new invertebrate - and let the bag float in the tank for 15 minutes.

2. Open the bag and place the invertebrate into a container with the bag water – ensuring the invertebrate stays covered with bag water.

    It is always a good idea to add an air stone to the container. This keeps the oxygen and pH levels high, and circulates the water in the container to lower stress and smooth acclimation.

3. Over the course of 30 minutes add a little water from the aquarium every 5 minutes to acclimate the invertebrate to your aquarium parameters.

    Steady/slow drip line from the tank works best.

4. Remove the invertebrate from the acclimation water, rinse it, and place it into the tank.

   It is often a good idea to assist new invertebrates to the bottom of the tank or rockwork using your hand. This keeps current inhabitants from thinking the new addition is food.

5. Keep the lights in the aquarium off for at least one hour to allow the new inhabitant to acclimate to the surroundings.

6. Watch your new and old livestock for compatibility issues – close for about ten minutes and every hour or so for the rest of the day.

   This should give you ample indication if they are not compatible.

Acclimating Anemones

1. Turn the lights off – to avoid cooking your new anemone - and float the anemone and bag inside the tank for 15 minutes.

2. Open the bag and place the anemone into a container with the bag water. Make sure the anemone is fully covered with water.

   It is always a good idea to add an air stone to the container. This keeps the oxygen and pH levels high, and circulates the water in the container to lower stress and smooth acclimation.

3. Over the course of 45 minutes add a little water from the aquarium every 5 minutes in order to acclimate the anemone to your water parameters.

   Steady/slow drip line from the tank works best

4. Turn the aquarium pumps off.

5. Using a vinyl or latex (non-powdered) glove, remove the anemone from the acclimation water and place it in a separate container of water from the aquarium.

   Make sure to use a flat palm under the anemone to move it outside the water. The tissue is easily damaged by the water weight it holds when fully inflated. I find an open palm or two works best.

   Allow it to soak for 1-3 minutes before placing it in the aquarium (Step 6).

   (Reason for gloves: Anaphylactic shock or even death can occur from the sting of some saltwater livestock – certainly the anemone is capable, if allergic. Most people are fine, but safety first.)

6. Using a vinyl or latex (non-powdered) glove, pick up the anemone and place it into the aquarium.

7. Hold the anemone – foot side down - very lightly to a rock for approximately 30 seconds.

The anemone foot will begin to attach. After it attaches slowly remove your hand.

8. Keep the pumps off for an additional 15-45 minutes to give the anemone time to fully attach.

9. After removing your hand from the tank, keep the lights in the aquarium off for at least one hour to allow the anemone to adjust to the surroundings.

10. Watch your new and old livestock for compatibility issues – close for about ten minutes and every hour or so for the rest of the day.

   This should give you ample indication if they are not compatible.

Acclimating Coral (Dip method)

It is recommended to dip coral in a solution of Revive® Coral Cleaner, Seachem® Reef Dip, or CoralRx®. These processes help ensure you don't bring home any unwanted pests.

1. Turn the lights off and float the coral – still in the bag – in the tank for 15 minutes.

2. Open the bag and place the coral and bag water into a container that will not be used for food.

Coral is extremely poisonous – never eat coral or use anything from coral for food.

It is always a good idea to add an air stone to the container. This keeps the oxygen and pH levels high, and circulates the water in the container to lower stress and smooth acclimation.

3. Over the course of 30 minutes add a little water every 5 minutes.

Steady/slow drip line from the tank works best

4. After you are done acclimating - mix the appropriate amount of coral dip with new/clean aquarium water and move the air stone to this new container.

5. Place the coral into the coral dip for 5-15 minutes. Take care to not damage skeleton or tissue. Damage may leave the coral prone to infection.

6. Take the coral out of the dip, rinse it, place it into the aquarium, then throw the dip water out.

Glue frags directly inside the tank using gel super glue.

Feeding the Aquarium

Saltwater aquariums require cleaner foods than freshwater aquariums. Most saltwater foods are also enriched with some type of vitamin or mineral to make it healthier for the livestock. These vitamins and minerals add to the coloration of your livestock and increase vibrancy over time. The basic types of food are liquid, pellet, flake, and frozen.

Liquid foods are usually used to feed corals, feather dusters, and other filter feeders. Not all corals require feeding, but all corals can filter feed. The problem with liquid foods is they add to the dissolved organics in the aquarium and form ammonia, nitrite, and nitrate. By following manufacturer instructions you can keep a lot of the excess nutrients out.

Pellet foods are my preferred method of feeding. Pellets are a healthy combination of foods for your livestock. Most pellets can feed everything from fish and invertebrates to coral. The pellets stay whole long enough for the fish and invertebrates to eat them – leaving less waste dissolve – and release small amounts of food particles into the water which can help nourish filter feeders.

Flake food is something I like to reserve for freshwater tanks. Experienced hobbyists do have luck with feeding it to smaller fish and filter feeders, but I don't like the way it breaks down in the water and gets stuck in the rocks. Remember, unconsumed foods break down into dissolved organics and turn into nitrate. Nitrate is poisonous to coral, and no good for reef tanks.

Frozen food is great and nutritious when used properly. Most people use too much frozen food, causing themselves headaches with water quality that lead to algae growth. Frozen food is better used as a treat than a daily food. It is also a good idea to thaw the food and remove any excess liquid before feeding the contents to the aquarium. This will limit dissolved organics in the water.

The main reasons you want to watch what you feed are: water quality, algae, and nutrients. The wrong food will not provide the right nutrients and minerals for the livestock. The right food, in too high a content, will cause bad water quality, which can lead to livestock death and excess algae growth. Ultimately, feeding is extremely important for your aquarium and should be done two to three times a day, just watch the quantity of food added.

Maintaining Your Tank

Saltwater aquariums require a lot of different types of maintenance, but they are all relatively easy.

Water changes, glass cleaning, siphoning debris, water testing, skimmer cleaning, sock cleaning or replacement, media replacement, and other cleaning are all part of a good maintenance regiment. It may sound like a lot, but in reality it is really not that hard.

Over time you will learn a schedule for your particular system, but until you have had the time to devise one that is best for you, here is a basic rundown on what you should accomplish with your maintenance schedule.

This chart shows a very basic maintenance schedule.

Daily Maintenance	Feeding	Cleaning the inside Glass	Topping off Freshwater
Weekly Maintenance	Sock Replacement or Cleaning	Skimmer Cleaning	Water Testing
Bi-Weekly Maintenance	20% Water Change	Siphon Out Debris	
Monthly Maintenance	Replace Media	Clean off Salt Creep	Trim Coral
Bi-Monthly Maintenance	Clean Pumps		
6 Month Maintenance	Replace Light Bulbs		

Following a schedule is likely to help you drastically in your endeavor to have a beautiful saltwater aquarium.

Feeding, cleaning the glass, and topping off freshwater are all daily tasks you will need to complete. The feeding part we have already discussed, but we have not talked about how you clean the glass or why you use freshwater to top off.

Glass can be cleaned with a magnetic scrubber or by use of a special sponge. Don't use anything not made for an aquarium because it could have harmful chemicals on it – this is especially true for dish sponges. You should do this daily to keep from having an obstructed view of the tank. Daily cleaning will also make it much easier to clean. After the algae has had days to build up, it tends to get much harder to remove.

You are going to need to top off you tank with freshwater, daily. This will help maintain the salinity level of the aquarium. **R**everse **O**smosis **D**e-ionized (RO/DI) water is the best to use for a saltwater tank. This water is extremely pure and void of any harmful metals or other organics. Salt does not evaporate so make sure you only top off with freshwater. You are doing this to maintain a stable salinity and replace what evaporated.

About once a week you are going to need to replace your filter sock, clean the skimmer, and test the water. A lot of people throw their socks away when they change them, but I recommend you wash and reuse them to save some money. Skimmer cleaning is a dirty and usually smelly job, but doing it weekly will help you maintain a happy tank. Water quality is one of the most important things so your water should be tested at least once a week.

When replacing the filter sock you should have one ready to put back in. Cutting the return pump off while replacing the sock can help cut down on the amount of water spilled in the process. I usually look down into my filter sock to ensure no fish or livestock has traveled down the overflow. There are normally amphipods and copepods in the sock, so don't be alarmed by the little bug things moving around in there.

Save your socks in a bucket with a capful of bleach and some RO/DI water. When you get enough you can wash them in the washing machine on hot with **no soap** (you can use bleach). Hang them dry and give a few days for the bleach to completely evaporate. Do this until they wear out – saving money.

Cleaning the skimmer is pretty easy. I usually remove the collection cup and place it into a bucket of used saltwater. This keeps from killing the bacteria on the skimmer. If you clean any of your parts in freshwater you will kill the good bacteria on them. Using your hands, rub the collection cup out and make sure you get everything off the inside. Excess gunk left on the skimmer walls will catch protein and allow it to fall back into the tank water.

Water testing should be done weekly – maybe even more frequently - by the inexperienced hobbyist. Just about any aquarium store worth its weight in salt (no pun intended) can test your water for free or cheap. I recommend taking water to the aquarium store for weekly testing. Weekly testing will help you maintain your water parameters and give you enough time to fix problems before they start.

On a bi-weekly basis you should do a 20% water change while siphoning out the detritus and other debris. This will help refresh the water quality, replace used trace elements, and remove unwanted nutrients like nitrate and phosphate. This can be done pretty easily using a small siphon hose and waste bucket. I describe the process in detail in the next section on water quality and water changes.

Replacement of carbon and phosphate media should be part of monthly maintenance. Carbon media removes dissolved organics from the water, reducing the yellow and or green water effect. Carbon media can also remove poisons which are injected into the tank by corals as a form of coral warfare.

Phosphate media comes in two types: aluminum oxide and ferric oxide. Aluminum oxide comes in small white balls of oxidized aluminum. The benefit to aluminum oxide is it removes silicates along with phosphates. Ferric oxide is what most people call rust. Ferric oxide removes phosphate, but does not remove silicates. It reacts faster than aluminum oxide. Both media should be replaced as used - generally once a month.

Salt creep is very dangerous. Aquarium fires can kill. Don't let this happen to you and your family. Salt creep is the buildup of salt on lights, pumps, fans, and anything else around the aquarium. It is very important to clean this salt off of your components and equipment at least once a month. Using freshwater and a rag is the easiest way to clean up salt creep, but sometimes it will require more specialized tools like a can of compressed air.

Salt is not only extremely corrosive, but it is a great conductor of electricity. Salt creep builds inside of electrical components and causes shorts. These shorts turn into full blown fires and should not be taken lightly. Don't forget to unplug anything electrical before you clean or remove it from the aquarium. Risk of electrocution around a saltwater aquarium is real.

I've had two aquarium lights catch fire on me. I can tell you first hand: it's scary – especially if you are sleeping or not home when it happens. Make sure you clean your components regularly and inspect for damage. Don't risk the lives of you, your family, or your neighbors.

Once a month – give or take a few weeks – the established reef should be trimmed down to keep the corals from killing each other. Most local reef stores will take the trimmings in trade and give you something in return. If a local store won't accept them in trade, you can always look for local hobbyists to trade with, but check local laws first.

Contrary to popular belief, coral trimming is very easy. I recommend looking for coral trimming/fragging videos online. There is a huge assortment of videos online about trimming and/or fragging coral. You can probably find a video about fragging each different type of coral in your tank. You may be amazed how easy it is to frag.

Every few months you will want to remove your pumps from the tank when doing a water change. This gives you tank water to clean them with. It also ensures you kill as little good bacteria as possible. Remove the pumps, open them up, and clean them out with a small scrubber. Most pet stores carry some type of pipe cleaning kit that can be useful for this task. Keeping the pumps clean will ensure adequate water flow and longevity of the pump.

If you think your pumps need a deep clean you can completely remove them from the system and clean them in a vinegar bath. White vinegar helps breakdown stubborn calcium deposits and will not harm your aquarium or the inhabitants. A lot of people also use white vinegar to clean the glass and overflow of a used tank before setting it back up.

Unless you have LEDs, you are going to have to replace your light bulbs about every six months. Over time our aquarium bulbs shift spectrum and no longer put out the wavelength of light we need. Not only does this affect the color of the light, but it affects coral and algae growth. Old bulbs can promote nuisance algae and inhibit coral. Replacing the bulbs every six months is recommended, but some hobbyists go up to a year.

Proper maintenance is extremely important for a healthy saltwater aquarium. The maintenance is not hard, and does not take much time, but there are a lot of things to do. Use the chart above to help remind yourself of when you need to do certain things. Add to the chart over time to make sure you don't miss anything your tank requires.

Let me reiterate one more time the importance of cleaning salt creep. Salt creep can cause fires that kill. Don't let your family or a neighbor lose everything including their lives because of failure to clean off salt creep. It is extremely important and should not be put off.

Water Testing Log Sheet

Keeping a log of your water testing will help solve problems before they happen. You can chart these results later for a graph of your tank parameters.

Date				
Time (AM | PM)				
pH				
Alkalinity (dKH | meq/l)				
Calcium (ppm)				
Magnesium (ppm)				
Nitrate (ppm)				
Nitrite (ppm)				
Phosphate (ppm)				
Ammonia (ppm)				
Salinity (Specific Gravity)				
Temperature (°F | °C)				

General Maintenance Log Sheet

Keeping a log of your maintenance will help you recognize issues early and maintain a more balanced reef. You can reference these results if you have irregularities or problems.

Task	Date Completed			
Cleaning Glass Inside and Outside				
Bulb Replacement				
Sock Change				
Skimmer Cleaning				
Water Change And Percent				
Media Replacement				
Top End Salt Creep Cleaning				
Bottom End Salt Creep Cleaning				
Siphoning out Detritus				
Trim Coral				
Pump Cleaning				

Specifics on Water and Water Quality

Water in your aquarium is one of the main three components. Without good water quality all of your efforts will be for nothing. It is easy to get confused about water and water quality. Choosing a salt to use for your tank shouldn't be taken lightly. I use a very specific salt and would not use anything else.

Why is water quality so important?

Marine life has gone millions of years without much change in water parameters. Most marine livestock does not do well with changing conditions because of this. Maintaining good water parameters with little fluctuation is vital to a healthy and happy aquarium.

How do I maintain water parameters?

The easiest way to maintain water parameters is through a good water change and water testing schedule. Water changes can replace used trace elements needed to maintain healthy livestock.

Regular testing will keep the hobbyist informed as to their water parameters, and let them know when something is wrong or needs correcting.

Ensure you use only the best salts and 0 tds RO/DI water to mix saltwater for water changes and for freshwater top off.

Water parameters can mean the difference between coral growth and coral recession. With the right water parameters you are many times less likely to have problems in your aquarium.

Good water parameters allow your livestock to be healthy and will increase the chance of fighting off infection from sicknesses and parasites.

Water Parameter Guidelines

These are the basic water parameter guidelines. Here are parameters for a fish only with live rock and for a reef tank.

	FOWLR	REEF
Ammonia	0 ppm	0 ppm
Nitrite	0 ppm	0 ppm
Nitrate	0-30 ppm	0-5 ppm
Phosphate	0-1 ppm	0-0.3 ppm
Temperature	72-78°	72-78°
S/G (Salinity)	1.021-1.023	1.024-1.025
Iodine	0.04-0.10 ppm	0.06-0.10 ppm
pH	8.1-8.4	8.1-8.4
Calcium	320-400 ppm	420-550 ppm
Alkalinity	8-11 dKH	10-14 dKH
Magnesium	1050-1350 ppm	1250-1400 ppm
Strontium	4-10 ppm	8-14 ppm
Potassium	380-400 ppm	390-420ppm

RO/DI Water System and Water

The first filter in a general 4 stage RO/DI system is the sediment filter. This filter removes solids from the water – dissolved and not dissolved.

After the sediment filter there is generally a carbon filter. The carbon filter will remove ammonia, chlorine, and other chemicals before the water reaches the RO Membrane. The removal of these chemicals protects the membrane from destruction.

The RO membrane removes most of the remaining contaminants and leaves the water at around 10 parts per million (ppm).

After exiting the RO membrane water heads to the DI resin chamber. The DI (Deionization Resin) removes the remaining solids and brings your PPM down to 0. This is far removed from the water entering the RO system at between 150 and 350PPM.

At 0 tds the water is ready to be used for top off or mixing saltwater. Using other water – with tds (total deposit of solids) might result in contaminants which can cause algae and stress/death to the aquarium inhabitants.

Picking a Salt

The main thing to consider when picking a salt is the type of aquarium. A fish only aquarium does not have the same requirements as a reef aquarium. Reef aquariums require a much higher level of elements like calcium and magnesium than a fish only system.

Most of the salts on the market referring to pro-reef or something similar are going to be your reef tank salts. General fish only aquariums only require regular salts because they don't use near as many trace elements as reef tanks.

The salt you choose is very important for the health of your reef and inhabitants. Research is the best tried and true way to find the right combination.

(Please also see - Pick Salt – at the end of the Chapter)

Mixing Saltwater

Reef tanks generally prefer salinity as high as 1.026, but I recommend keeping the salinity at 1.024-1.025. This gives the new hobbyist a margin of error in salinity to accommodate evaporation.

Fish only aquariums can have a lower level of salt in the water. It is recommended to keep the salinity from 1.021-1.023 for fish only systems. Some advanced hobbyists keep their salinity lower to stem back parasitic infections, but this should not be done by the beginner.

How often do I change the water?

For the sake of simplicity you should do bi-weekly water changes. These regularly scheduled water changes will help promote a clean and healthy environment for your reef aquarium. I recommend you change out 20% of your water every two weeks. This will remove enough water to take out some contaminants while refreshing enough trace elements to help your livestock thrive.

Best way to do a water change

The best way to do a water change is to allow your new saltwater to acclimate to the temperature of the room and then turn off all pumps in the aquarium. Using a siphon tube seems to work the best for me when removing water. A small diameter siphon hose can be used to clean while changing the water.

The easiest way to start a siphon is to fill the siphon tube with aquarium water, plug the ends, put one end down to the waste reservoir while leaving the other end in the tank, and let both ends loose. If you have done it right then the hose should have been completely filled with water before releasing the two ends and the siphon should start automatically. This removes the risk of getting a mouth full of water.

If you use a small diameter siphon hose you can clean the aquarium of detritus and other debris while doing your water change. This can drastically improve water quality over time. While holding one end of the siphon hose in your waste bucket use small rapid circles with the other end of the hose kick up debris and suck it out.

After 20% of the water has been removed you will want to use a spare pump to add the water back to your aquarium. Once you have completed this process you will want to turn the pumps back on. Dump the old water into your drain or set it out to evaporate and dispose of the salt in the garbage.

I find filling the top of the tank to the point it starts to overflow down to the sump is a good way to refill the tank to the point it was at before I began. Some people I have spoken with like to use five gallon buckets to remove water and to add it back. This gives them the ability to count the exact number of gallons. With a little practice you will find the method that best suits you.

Water Flow

Water flow in a saltwater aquarium is extremely important because it dictates the oxygen level in the water and around the corals, fish, and invertebrates. All corals and most invertebrates get their oxygen through absorption. If the water does not move around them enough they will suffocate and die. Likewise, fish require a lot of oxygen and can quickly run out if there is not a continual flow from outside of the tank.

Flow rate includes the return pump along with any other pumps in the tank. Adding the flow rate of these pumps brings you the total flow rate.

Hobbyists have learned over the years to use a flow rate at between twenty and thirty times the tank volume per hour. See the chart below for flow rates for general tank sizes.

Tank Size	Fish Only (x20) Gallons Per Hour	Reef Tank (x30) Gallons Per Hour
10	200	300
20	400	600
30	600	900
40	800	1200
55	1100	1650
65	1300	1950
75	1500	2250
90	1800	2700
125	2500	3750
150	3000	4500
180	3600	5400
220	4400	6600

By keeping your flow in line with this flow chart you are much more likely to have adequate oxygen levels in your aquarium for all of the inhabitants. Proper oxygen levels will help keep your livestock healthy. Remember, these are general figures and not an exact match. These ranges are a starting point and may change depending on your specific aquarium needs.

Different Salts

Using a good salt will show up in your testing. Better salts show better results immediately and over time.

Good salts have a lot more minerals in them. This helps stabilize the system over time. It decreases pH fluctuations and maintains oxygen levels. Using a good salt also ensures few impurities in your aquarium.

I advocate for quality salt wherever possible. Quality saltwater helps ensure health, longevity, and rapid growth rates.

Lower quality salts are often acceptable for fish only systems. These lower cost salts tend to come with decreased amounts of minerals and lower quality controls. This causes a range of possible mixture levels and can stress livestock over time.

If you buy your saltwater premixed from your local store, make sure to ask them exactly what salt they use to mix your water, and what levels it tests at.

Next time you buy water for a water change, take your new water out to the car/truck and fill a sample container to have tested. Then, walk right back into the store and have them test the sample for you. This will give you a more accurate reading of the quality. Don't tell them it's theirs until after they test it for you.

D0: Right after a water change   D=Day
D7: One week after water change
D14: Right before water change

Day 0-14	D0	D7	D14
Calcium:	350ppm	300ppm	300ppm

Cheap Salt:

(It is hard to find a tank below 300ppm, even if it has not been maintained. Calcium seems too slow in uptake around this number – at least in my experience)

Magnesium:	950ppm	900ppm	850ppm

(I don't think I have seen magnesium this low no matter the maintenance level of the tank. It seems to be a low spot in magnesium for saltwater. I would assume that lower levels generally come from tanks that reach this point and top off with freshwater diluting the levels to below their minimum threshold for uptake. I would consider them outliers.)

Alkalinity:	7.4 dkH	6.0dkH	5.0dkH

(This is also a low level I rarely see. This number generally indicates a tank that has not gotten the care that it desires, but finds this level to stay around. Sometimes it can be worse, but it is usually due to dosing errors that bring the alkalinity down to a lower level than it would normally travel to.)

pH:	8.0	7.7	7.4

(If your pH is this low you can see signs of stress on your livestock. Fish will appear to be pale and corals will either recede to save oxygen or will blow up like a balloon to get more oxygen out of the water. pH and oxygen are related to each other, and generally (without intervention) will stabilize at a low level like this. Even with low alkalinity you can maintain your pH using air stones, water circulation, surface agitation, and more. The trick is to not need to.)

Bad salt could also affect nitrates and phosphates, but they were left off for ease of explanation.

Good Salt:

Day 0-14	D0	D7	D14
Calcium:	600ppm	530ppm	480ppm

(Even though this number may not be my target number, it stays well above the recommended minimum levels.)

Magnesium:	1350ppm	1310ppm	1270ppm

(This is a healthy dose above what the recommended minimums are.)

Alkalinity:	10.2 dkH	9.7 dkH	9.0 dkH

(9.0 is well above the recommended low level. This higher level will help maintain oxygen levels, keep out unwanted algae, and help your corals solidify the calcium, magnesium, strontium, and more in the tank for growth.)

pH:	8.4	8.1	7.8

(This is not exactly at the recommended level of 8.1-8.4, but the small points from 7.8 to 7.4 do matter quite a bit. It matters a lot more because of the pH swing that happens when most people are not testing their tanks: at night. Swings of a whole point are possible at night. This can increase stress and cause livestock sickness.)

Dosing is always an option for maintaining levels of trace elements. This method lets you increase the parameters or just keep them steady. The problem I have with dosing is chemicals are expensive and rarely give the same variety of trace elements as a good salt. Lacking in trace elements can cause severe stress and even death to inhabitants.

Not only is a good salt easier to maintain the general side of the tank, it can also make other maintenance tasks easier. For instance, good pH and high alkalinity can stem back algae growth. By starving the algae for the right parameters you can cause it to grow slower, or not at all.

Selecting Healthy Livestock

Picking Livestock

When at the store there are things you will want to watch out for while picking your livestock. I wish I could say all stores sell only healthy livestock, but the truth is a lot of employees don't even know what to look for, if they even care to tell you. Though you can never tell if a piece of livestock is completely healthy, we will briefly discuss what to look for in fish, coral, invertebrates, and anemones.

One of the most important things to do is make sure a fish is eating. Make sure there are no spots on the fish – either black or white – as they could be signs of black or regular ich. If the fish rubs on the rocks, sand, or walls of the tank, it could also be a sign of external parasites.

Lethargic fish should be avoided as it is a sign of general ill health. Make sure the fish does not have any bulging areas which could be signs of bacterial infection. Raised scales and bare tissue can also be signs of bacterial and fungal infection. The last thing to watch for is cloudy eyes. Cloudy eyes can be a sign of internal parasites.

When purchasing coral you will want to watch out for a few things. White or transparent coral is a sign of ill health. Most transparent coral has lost the zoanthelle algae inside and is going to die. Rarely can this coral be brought back. Watch out for corals that appear to be receding as this is a sign of eventual death or poor water quality. Lastly, if a coral does not open completely, it should be avoided. It may be a sign of some type of parasite or ill health.

It is much harder to tell the health of invertebrates. I recommend asking to see some invertebrates eat. This is not possible for all of them, but should be done with shrimp and crabs at the least.

Lethargic invertebrates which lie on the bottom or don't move should be avoided. Pale invertebrates may be molting and should not be moved until a few days after the molt. The soft shell underneath the molt is extremely sensitive to damage and leaves the livestock vulnerable to sickness and predators.

Invertebrates rarely get diseases or parasites that we know of, so the general health of them is what you should be looking for.

It is generally very easy to tell the health of anemones. They have certain telltale signs you can look for. Just like coral, anemones should have good coloration. Anemones that are clear and or white should be avoided. Shriveled up anemones should be avoided as it could be a sign of death. Anemones should be well inflated when healthy.

Healthy anemones will be well attached to the substrate, rock, or glass in the tank. The last thing to look for in anemones is the mouth size. Healthy anemones will have a very small mouth, whereas unhealthy anemones can turn inside out from the mouth. This looks a lot like the anemone foot, but on top.

I don't recommend anything other than bubble anemones for the inexperienced hobbyist. As you get further advanced and learn more about the anemones you can purchase other types. If an anemone dies in your tank it can kill everything. It is wise to be cautious when purchasing an anemone.

Fish Quarantine and Coral Dips

Quarantine and dips are the only ways to ensure your reef will stay healthy. About 99% of the crashes in saltwater tanks could have been avoided with proper quarantine and dip procedures. I recommend setting up a quarantine tank for your fish and using dips for corals. We will briefly discuss them both here.

Quarantine tanks are aquariums setup for the purpose of watching livestock for a period of time ranging from a few days to a few weeks before putting them in the main display. Most hobbyists keep copper in their fish quarantine system to kill external parasites while the fish is in quarantine.

I highly recommend setting up a quarantine tank for fish with copper. You should quarantine any fish you get for at least seven days, but I recommend nine. This gives you enough time to see if the fish has any health issues that you don't want to introduce to your main display.

Every time we sold coral in my store we offered free coral dip. It is always wise to dip every coral, every time. Most stores don't mention coral dip, let alone offer free samples. I think coral dip is vital to a happy and healthy reef tank.

Coral dip kills parasites that can hitchhike on corals. The dips can kill flatworms, redbugs, nudibranch, and more. We dipped every coral coming in the store and we still gave dip away for free.

Even with dipping you can acquire some types of parasite in your tank. You would be wise to dip every coral, every time. Every coral, every time. Every coral, every time. Once more, every coral, every time. Did you get that? Every coral, every time.

Back to Basics Recap

Let's recap a little here. We started out discussing what is required to own a saltwater aquarium. Basically, this comes down to proper maintenance and a little time. Some tanks take more time and money than others. This is usually related to the size of the tank, but can also relate to the sanity of the hobbyist – in other words the amount of time they are willing to spend.

Next, we discussed the aquarium setup and cycle. We talked about the order in setting up an aquarium, the biological filtration, and the nitrogen cycle. Your aquarium is its own eco-system and requires a biological filter to maintain a healthy environment for the livestock. Most saltwater aquarium cycles take between four and eight weeks.

Introducing livestock is a delicate process. You should always acclimate livestock properly and save yourself a headache by having a good quarantine and dip process. This will work about 99% of the time to keep your main display free of parasites and other problems.

Feeding your aquarium properly is very important for water quality and livestock health. You should feed up to three times a day, but keep it in moderation. You don't want to cause unneeded nitrates and phosphates.

Following a few simple maintenance procedures can help you maintain your tank with ease. If you keep the tank and water clean, you are far more likely to have success.

Water quality, lighting, and flow are the three most important ingredients to a healthy reef tank. Make sure your water parameters follow a good guide like the one in the section on water quality. Also, keep your water parameters steady, because fluctuating parameters are bad for livestock.

The right type of light is vital to the growth of coral. Most of it grows deep enough below the ocean surface to reflect back most light.

Flow in your tank should be between twenty and thirty times the tank volume, per hour. This will ensure adequate water flow around your corals, fish, and invertebrates, and provide the right amounts of oxygen.

Above all else, remember, this is a hobby. You are supposed to enjoy it. It is amazing and fun, but can seem daunting at times. My hope is this book will save you lots of money, headaches, and time. Best of luck!

Check out some of the following pages for a small number of tips and tidbits I found interesting enough to put up around my store.

Tips and More

Feeding

What you feed and how often you feed are both vital to the health of your aquarium inhabitants. That includes imperative microbes you can't see.

Frozen foods should be fed as a treat and should be drained well before feeding. Excess liquid from frozen foods gets trapped in the water and adds to nitrate and phosphate levels.

Flake food should be fed sparingly. It can get trapped in the rockwork and filter system. This causes a nitrate and phosphate increase.

It is recommended to feed a balanced diet of quality pellet food with a mix of frozen and other supplements.

How your corals look (Color etc..)

The main reason for a hobbyist to have problems with coral coloration is lighting. Coral is very picky when it comes to light spectrum. Only certain frequencies of light make it deep enough under the water to reach coral.

When we purchase aquarium lighting it is designed to produce that wavelength. Lights can get old and shift spectrum.

Ultravoilet light causes coral to produce a thin protective coating that reflects light – this usually results in a "neon glow" under blue light.

Tangs, Damsels, Gobies, and Ich

Tangs and other open ocean swimmers are more likely to get ich because they have a thinner slime coating due to their need for speed in the open water. They move so fast in the open ocean that there is less protection needed. They never stay still long enough for an ich parasite to latch onto them.

Anemone fish (including clownfish) are a type of damsel. Damsels spend considerable time hosting anemones when they are young. Later, many abandon the host and travel the reef.

Clownfish, on the other hand, tend to stay paired with anemones their entire lives. This is only possible for them because of an increased thickness in their slime coating which makes them less likely to get ich.

Many gobies have a dense skin or scale layer and are very unlikely to get ich, except inside their gills.

The best way to keep from getting ich is healthy tank feeding and cleaning habits, along with proper acclimation procedures.

Coral Dip

There are many different types of coral dip, but they all do basically the same thing – or so they say. Coral dips are designed to heal coral and kill parasites.

The reason we dip when we purchase is to clean the coral of any possible pests before the coral goes into our system. "An ounce of prevention" is worth several pounds of cure in this case.

It is still possible for eggs to get through coral dip, so inspect the piece well before introducing it into the aquarium.

The other reason to use coral dip is to heal an infected coral. Iodine based dips can speed healing time and kill off bacterial infections.

How does an RO/DI unit work?

Water quality coming into the home fluctuates depending on location in the world, but it is usually around 100 to 300 tds (total deposit of solids). This water then enters the RO/DI unit and goes through a sediment filter. This filter removes everything from the water down to 1 micron.

After traveling through the sediment filter, the water goes into a carbon filter. This is where dissolved organics and chemicals like chlorine are removed. The removal of these chemicals helps ensure the long life of the membrane.

Once the water leaves the carbon block it enters the membrane where osmosis brings the tds down to a level between 0 and 20. Lower is better. Wastewater comes out of the membrane around 3 times as fast as clean water.

From this point the water moves into the DI resin. The resin removes the remaining solids in the water. The water comes out now at 0 tds. This water is ready to be used for top off or salt mixing.

Change your carbon filter every 300-400 gallons of clean water produced in order to protect your membrane. The membrane should last up to a year if well taken care of.

Water Temperature Changes Kill Livestock

Keeping a steady water temperature is actually more important than the exact temperature. Saltwater livestock generally does best in water temperatures of 72 to 76 degrees Fahrenheit. More important than the exact temperature is the stability of the temperature.

Fluctuations in water temperature can cause oxygen levels to go up and down – leaving the livestock in the system with inadequate oxygen levels and possibly toxic carbon dioxide levels. The fish usually show the first signs with pale coloration and lethargic movement patterns. Fish are likely to die first when oxygen drops below safe levels.

To keep oxygen levels up, do regular water changes, regular water testing, and maintain agitation of the water at the surface using return and circulation pumps. Oxygen level increases will also help lift and maintain pH.

Refugiums

There are many reasons to use a refugium in your saltwater aquarium - be it a reef, a fish only, or a predator tank. I'm convinced every aquarium can benefit from a refugium. This section will illustrate how the components of a refugium and what they do.

Whether you are having a problem with excess nutrients, nitrates, ph level, or slow copepod growth, a refugium may help. Refugiums clean your water of particulate, remove harmful nutrients, remove harmful protein, help oxygenate the water, maintain PH, grow copepods, clear out micro bubbles, turn nitrate into nitrogen for a completed cycle, and might even release trace elements into your water. These things help us create a better and more stable ecosystem.

We start with a bare water tight container:

This starts as nothing more than a box capable of holding water and ends up one of the best saltwater filters your aquarium can have. It's also eco-friendly. The size of your refugium is going to depend on your needs and space available. Not everyone will want to build this refugium for the same reason, so tailor this to your requirements.

The first stop for water is the sock:

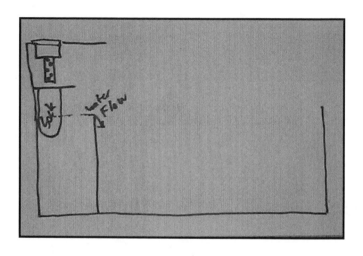

The water flows from the aquarium via gravity feed down a pipe to the refugium. Once the water hits the refugium it encounters the aquarium sock(s) (seen here on the left in my crude drawing). The sock is a great way to remove particles from the aquarium. Aquarium socks are generally available in 200 micron, but I have seen them as fine as 100 micron. The finer socks do a better job of removing smaller particulate, but need to be changed more often.

Socks become nitrate sponges if not changed regularly. I recommend changing socks at least once every two weeks – every week is better. When you clean socks, run them through the wash *without* soap. It is okay to use bleach. After using bleach, give 3-5 days for air drying before use. This will help remove trace amounts of chlorine.

Socks are usually set up at the beginning of a refugium. This is usually the easiest way to ensure the water gets filtered through the sock, but it doesn't remove copepods and amphipods from the refugium. The sock also helps ensure debris doesn't build up in the first few chambers.

When water leaves the sock chamber it pours over the baffle like a waterfall into the skimmer chamber:

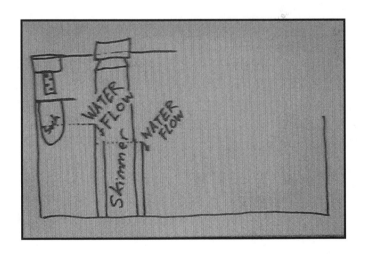

There are several reasons why we want a skimmer. Skimmers remove all kinds of proteins, such as, fish waste, bacteria, and free floating algae. This purification helps keep the water crystal clear so the lights can penetrate deeper. Skimmers can also add oxygen to the water.

There are draw backs to using a skimmer that is too large. Overrated skimmers can remove trace elements and vitamins. It can also result in stress to livestock. Basically, the skimmer can removes trace elements and minerals before the livestock – including coral, fish, and invertebrates – have the chance to absorb them.

You will most likely want to place the skimmer in the second chamber. The skimmer will produce micro-bubbles bind with proteins in the water and draw them to the surface for collection. Some of these micro-bubbles escape the skimmer and can end up in your display tank. Placing it before the refugium part helps catch left over micro-bubbles and gives them time to escape before the water returns to the aquarium.

You will want to clean your skimmer about once a week. The longer you wait the less it will remove. When proteins start building up on the inside walls of the collection cup, less waste makes it into collection.

Clean the skimmer on a separate schedule from your socks. Many socks and skimmers host a portion of the biological filtration. Changing both at once might cause a mini cycle.

I like to clean my skimmer and permanent equipment when I do a water change. That way you can utilize the wastewater for scrubbing and rinsing without killing the entire biological filter. (Freshwater kills bio-filters).

Next chamber in line is the actual refugium part of the Ultimate Refugium:

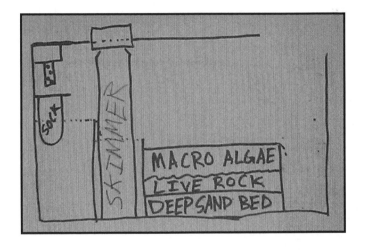

The refugium center is where all the magic happens... well, most of the magic happens here. This is where we can put a deep sand bed, rubble rock, and chaeto. Some people like to put invertebrates in this chamber. If there is a fish or invertebrate you really want, but can't keep in the display, this may be a good place for it.

Okay, so the refugium section helps remove micro-bubbles; we know this already. It also holds macro algae like chaeto, which removes nitrates and phosphates.

Macro algae use the nitrates and phosphates to grow. When you trim the macro algae back, it removes the nitrates and phosphates from the system. Chaeto can also provide a good location for copepod growth – helping feed the aquarium live food.

Deep sand beds are also very beneficial to the saltwater ecosystem. They provide a beneficial hypoxic area that grows nitrate eating bacteria. The end result of this nitrate eating process is nitrogen. The nitrogen bubbles up and out of the water and the nitrate cycle is complete. You are left with cleaner water for your inhabitants. If argonite is used in the deep sand bed it can release calcium carbonate - buffering pH and helping maintain calcium levels.

The average refugium also houses live rubble rock. This gives more surface area for beneficial nitrifying bacteria, sponge, and copepods to grow. Sponge filters nutrients and other impurities from the water. Copepods eat detritus and help feed the main display.

Properly timed refugiums balance PH throughout the day and night. Setting your refugium light opposite your display tank, can help remove carbon dioxide at night, releasing oxygen in the process. This inverse lighting from the main display light will help maintain a stable pH. Most aquariums have pH fluctuations at night, resulting in depleted oxygen levels and stress on the inhabitants.

The refugium helps remove micro-bubbles, ammonia, nitrite, nitrate, phosphate, and other impurities. It provides a refuge for copepods, amphipods, and baby starfish. They help maintain pH (and oxygen levels) in your aquarium at night. There are many benefits to using a refugium on your tank.

The return pump chamber is next on the list:

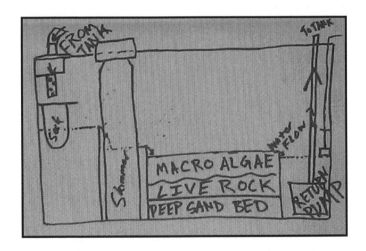

Once the water leaves the refugium it is time to push it back to our main display. Some people like to add a bubble catch at this point.

In this graphic you can see where the water enters the system at the sock. Then, it flows down a baffle into the skimmer chamber. Here it undergoes a second level of filtration before entering the refugium chamber.

The refugium chamber removes waste and acts as a location for copepod and other bio-filtration to take refuge. Then it trickles into the return pump chamber.

From there it gets sent back up to the main display – cleaner and complete with copepods.

See below for a refugium with bubble trap:

The bubble catch will remove any micro-bubbles that made it through the refugium chamber. This ensures a clean and clear display tank.

The return pump chamber is where you will want to add your auto top off system. The ATO can be purchased or built. The reason you want an ATO here instead of elsewhere is because it's the only location in your entire system where the water level will change with evaporation. I recommend placing the RO water fill host into the sock chamber.

In order to decide upon a bubble catch at the end of your system you should consider a few different things. First, the bubble catch will only be useful if there are actually bubbles getting by the refugium. Second, the bubble catch can act as a last resort for any livestock which climbs out of the refugium toward the pump. Finally, a bubble catch can remove space from the refugium or return chamber.

Each hobbyist will have to weigh this and other decisions on the needs of their system.

The following diagram shows the location of baffles. A) Sock chamber, B) Skimmer chamber, C) Refugium chamber, D/E) Bubble catch to return chamber:

The different chambers add different types of filtration. Some people like to add a media reactor to this type of setup. Usually this reactor sucks out of the refugium or return chamber and pumps back into the sump near the sock.

You can play around with the layout on a refugium or sump depending on your needs. There are many different types of layouts for a filtration system like this one. This is just my favorite.

You may also want sock and float switch mounts:

Sock mounts are basically a piece of plexiglass with a hole big enough to fit a sock. This is mounted near the top of the first chamber.

The float switch mount is constructed the same way, but is quite a bit smaller and only large enough to hold a float switch. Float switches should be mounted in the chamber with the return pump.

No design is going to be perfect for all hobbyists. You will have to figure out what is going to work for your system and livestock.

Refugiums: Build or Buy?

It used to be hobbyists had to build refugiums if they wanted one for their aquarium. The aquarium industry caught on and now sells sumps with built in refugiums.

You have a lot less ability to design the dimensions of a store bought refugium. This might mean it won't fit the exact needs of your system. Therefore, it may be better to build our own if your abilities and time permit.

I'm not saying a store bought refugium is always bad. There are several positives that go along with a mass produced system. Purchased refugiums are generally predesigned for certain tank sizes. This takes a lot of guesswork out of coming up with the dimensions of the sump. They are also ready to go when they arrive - just add livestock and water.

Building a refugium on the other hand requires a little more thought and time. By building your own you might be able to save 75% of the cost. There are usually old aquariums that can be used for sale on forums.

These old tanks can be used to make our refugium. Looks don't normally matter, but making sure it doesn't leak does matter. You might be able to pick one up free if you look hard enough. I generally use the largest aquarium I can fit while still leaving room for all my wiring.

Your refugium – should you decide to have one – will probably be different than mine. Keep this information in mind when you design your refugium. Each will change with different ecosystems, but they will all have the same basics.

Some people get creative with refugiums and make them a separate part of the display. This makes for a second interesting talking piece. Larger refugiums can be an ecosystem of their own. With the addition of mangroves, these systems can get very complicated and beautiful.

How to Move a Tank

So, you need to move a tank. This is quite the feat, but with a little reading you can make it go relatively smooth. Moving a system is a slow process, but it isn't near as hard as people think. There are some tricks about the process that will help greatly.

You may want to acquire some extra gear for the job. Totes (I use these super heavy duty ones from home depot), pump and hose (usually supplied by the current tank owner), a truck or trailer, and some friends you can talk into helping. If you can acquire these things before you even start it will go much easier.

The process starts with figuring out how many totes you are going to need. You can roughly figure this out according to the gallons of water the tank holds. Totes during transportation can usually hold around 50% of the water they are rated for. Any more than this and you are likely to lose water on the way home.

A 150 gallon aquarium requires almost 300 gallons worth of totes. You can also use a 55 gallon drum to hold water. I prefer to only take a tote per 50 gallons of tank size. This is enough for me to move the livestock and some of the rock without bringing all the water home. I refill with at least 50% freshly mixed saltwater.

The next thing I do is take pictures of everything. This will give you a blueprint to reply on when you are putting it back together. Don't hesitate to ask the old owner questions when you are breaking down the tank. Most hobbyists have put a lot of time and love into their tanks and they are happy to help you understand the care requirements.

From here you want to turning off all the pumps and draining some water into enough totes to hold the coral, live rock, fish, and invertebrates. Then, carefully remove any coral and place it in totes for safe travel. I like to add a battery operated air pump to the water at this point.

Careful to ensure the coral does not get crushed by rocks and does not touch other coral.

Once all of the coral is out of the display tank, you can start removing the liverock and placing it into containers. Do not remove the rock stuck in the sand yet. You want to get as much of the rock out of the tank as you can without stirring up the debris.

Once the rock is all removed you can catch the fish and invertebrates and place them in a tote of their own. Placing rock and coral in with fish and invertebrates can harm the fish and invertebrates when things shift on the drive home.

Before removing the half buried base rock, you should take out as much of the remaining water as you can. This water can be used to cover the base rock and some can be used to clean the sand before it goes back into the tank.

Next, remove the base rock and place it in a tote. Take the sand out and place it in totes without water. You need to keep the sand moist in order to kill as little of the bacteria as possible.

Make sure the water from the sump is also drained. The sump/refugium can hold a considerable amount of water. The stand should be emptied and crank straps should be used to hold the tank on the dolly. Extreme care should be taken for safety around large tanks. The glass is not forgiving when it breaks and can easily take a life. Always use caution.

Place the tank and stand on a furniture dolly and move it outside. Be very careful as they are extremely heavy. No tank over 120 gallons should be picked up by two people alone. My rule of thumb is a person per 60 gallon increment. I know a lot of people that didn't heed this advice. They have back problems now.

Move everything to the vehicle for transport, taking care not to leave it exposed to extreme temperatures for very long. Saltwater Livestock is very susceptible to changes in parameters and conditions. You want to get it to the new location and inside as soon as possible.

Keeping an air stone on the livestock for the trip will help make the experience less stressful.

The process for setting the tank back up is the same as taking it down, but slower. Use some of the water you got out of the tank to clean the sand and live rock before you put it into the tank.

Sand gets filthy over time and should definitely be sifted and cleaned. In many cases it should be completely replaced. Using the old saltwater to clean the sand will help keep the bacteria alive and shorten the length of time your mini cycle is going to take.

When putting a tank back together, I prefer to put an eggcrate down on the glass before the sand goes in, but that is just my preference. The order for me goes like this: eggcrate, sand, base rock, some water, live rock, some water, coral, remaining old clean water, fish and invertebrates, and any new saltwater needed to top off the water lost in transit.

The tank will probably be cloudy for at least a few days. This is the mini cycle your aquarium is going through because of the bacteria and algae die off in transition. You should pay close attention to the ammonia, nitrite, and nitrate levels during this period. Test everyday for a week or two. Spikes in these chemicals are deadly to livestock.

Local Markets

It is a good idea to check out the local markets before you make any purchases. Every market is a bit different. The best places I have found to check are forums, craigslist, and local pet shops. Local markets can decide how your budget is spent.

Forums are a great place to check for pricing. Saltwater aquarium forums usually have a place for members to sell and trade. This is a prime location to look for pricing. You can get involved in the forum and meet some great reefers. Sometimes, you can even pick up really cheap or free gear from online groups.

Craigslist is a location many people frequent to sell their goods and services. You can search craigslist for aquariums. I tend to pull up quite the number of listings every time I look. Scroll down the list and see what is available. Consider what is in the tank and how much you might be able to sell excess gear and livestock for.

Some local pet stores run sales where you can acquire a tank and stand very cheap. Even if they don't do this, there are some local establishments with forums you can search to locate personal tanks for sale.

Local stores are also a great place to meet other hobbyists and talk about reef-keeping. If nothing else, you can at least find out the cost of a new aquarium system. This will help you make purchasing decisions when you are ready to buy.

Local markets will ultimately decide the lowest price you can get. Shipping tanks is very expensive last I checked. Don't buy the first tank you see, because it will probably be a mistake – maybe not, but generally.

Consider checking more than just forums, craigslist, and local stores. When someone sits on a tank for a few months they get very eager to deal.

With your research complete, it is time to find a tank. You will have a better idea of what you are buying. If you are careful you can even make some money back on the equipment and livestock you don't want to keep.

Don't be afraid to consider buying it in pieces, waiting for a good deal, and haggling with sellers. I know people who buy two or three tanks, put one together, and sell the rest for a profit. It's a lot of work, but it can pay for itself.

This is your tank. You are going to be stuck with it. Make sure you get the one you really want. Your research should tell you what to offer the seller and what a fair value is. With a little research you can save a lot of time and maybe make some money in the process.

Marine Ich

What is ich?

Saltwater ich is a parasite known as *Cryptocaryon irritans.* This parasite has a three stage life cycle. It starts out as a small free swimming larvae looking for a host, then it attaches to the host and gains mass and maturity, after which it drops into the substrate and matures into a bursting larval hatchery.

What is the life cycle of ich?

The lifecycle of this parasite is generally between 7 and 72 days. Generally, these parasites have a maximum of a 28 day life cycle. Starting as a cyst and ending as a cyst hatchery, this parasite can multiply extremely fast in the aquarium.

My tank had ich, but it is completely gone now. Should I worry?

Most hobbyist think that ich has left their tank simply because they can't see the parasite on the fish anymore. This is not necessarily true. Fish build up a mucous layer defense against ich infestation when they are healthy and might not show visible signs of infection when in fact they are still infected.

Complete removal of fish for 72 days without any new addition of livestock is the only way to be 99.99% sure you are ich free.

My fish had ich, but it just went away.

It is a common misconception that ich can just go away. It might not show to the naked eye on a fish, but by no means does that imply it is gone.

The only stage of the ich lifecycle where you can see the parasite with a naked eye is when it's firmly implanted in the side of a fish, bursting with larval eggs, ready to drop into the substrate. The larval stage and cyst hatchery stage can not be seen by the naked eye.

All my fish were completely clean from ich, but I added a fish and now everything has ich. Why?

Ich might be present in the aquarium, but not visible because the fish have built up a relative immunity to the parasite. This might not completely stop marine ich from being present in the tank, but it keeps the parasite at bay.

The addition of a new fish provides a host that does not have the immunity, is stressed out, and has its immune defenses down from transfer. This new host allows the ich parasite to attach, gorge, and reproduce into hundreds or thousands of new parasites.

Why doesn't ich kill fish in the ocean?

In the ocean almost 99.9% of fish are infected with ich. The reason we don't notice the infections and fish are not dying from ich is because the waters are so widely open that the parasites rarely find the same hosts. With each fish carrying only a few parasites there is not enough damage to kill the fish or even cause any visual signs of the infection.

The confined space inside an aquarium allows the parasite to swarm in massive numbers around a few unlucky confined fish (kind of like the difference between being in the woods with snakes and being in a glass cage with all the snakes in the woods).

Because all fish from the ocean are infected, it is likely most fish in captivity are infected, and likely that your aquarium is also infected with the parasite.

Only one of my fish is infected, can I remove and treat him only?

If one fish in the aquarium is infected then it is almost certain all other fish in the aquarium are infected. Just because a fish does not show signs of infection does not mean they are not infected. Carriers of the parasite often show no signs until the infection has grown to massive proportion.

Can I just buy some cleaner shrimp or cleaner fish to get rid of it?

Cleaner shrimp and cleaner fish will not cure your fish of ich. The shrimp and fish will remove dead tissue and some parasites from your fish, but they are not an end all cure for the parasite. The only definite cure for ich is copper treatment.

How did I get ich?

The most common way to get ich is from an infected fish. The other way you can get ich is from the addition of water with the parasitic larva. This water can come from bags of water, and even the water on invertebrates or coral. Not even store bought water is completely safe from possible ich.

It is always a good practice to dip coral in coral dip and saltwater bathe invertebrates before placing them into the display.

How can I treat ich?

The only sure fire tried and true method for treating marine ich is through the use of copper. Copper is harmful to invertebrates and coral, so it can't be used in the reef tank.

Copper can also disrupt the biological filtration in an aquarium and should be raised slowly over a week or more to prevent a cycle or ammonia spike.

There are many "treatments" sold to hobbyists, but copper is the only one that has been time tested to continue working. Treatment with copper should be done in a hospital tank.

Different types of copper and the level to treat at with them.

There are many different copper treatments out there. I always recommend to people that they follow the manufacturer instructions for copper levels.

The same goes for anything you are going to dose in your tank. Always test and work to hit the target recommended level.

Things to remember:

You are not the first one to come down with saltwater ich. Because nearly 100% of all fish in the ocean carry marine ich, it is likely any fish you get will be infected if the proper precautions are not taken.

Ich has only one tried and true treatment: copper. Cleaner fish and cleaner shrimp may eat dead tissue and parasites from fish, but they are not going to cure your fish of ich. Just because a fish doesn't look like it has ich does not mean it's not a carrier.

Ich has three stages: larva, parasite, and larval hatchery. The only time ich is visible on the fish is during the parasitic stage.

Stressed fish are more susceptible to ich. This is something nearly every hobbyist has dealt with at one point or another. The important thing is to treat it early, before a problem occurs. Ask your local store to help guide you through the process of treating marine ich.

Do I Need Invertebrates?

Reef aquariums should have - on average - one hermit crab and one snail per gallon. This is just a general rule of thumb. Each tank is slightly different.

There are many different types of crabs, snails, and other invertebrates. Everything has a purpose in a reef aquarium. Keeping the right concentrations of invertebrates in your tank can help ensure a long and happy life for your ecosystem.

What kind of hermit crabs are best?

I recommend you get a variety of hermit crabs – blue legs, red legs, and white legs. Having a good hermit mix allows for a more versatile cleanup crew. Hermits not only clean during the day, but if anything in the aquarium happens to die, your hermits will be the first cleaners on the scene getting rid of the body.

All before it turns into ammonia and kills the other inhabitants. You should maintain the hermit population at a minimum of one hermit per gallon and a maximum of 1.5 hermits per gallon.

What type of snails should I have?

There are so many different types of snails – each having a specialty of their own. General turbo snails are great at keeping the rocks clean of excess algae and should be in a concentration of about one per gallon.

Mexican turbo snails are some of the very best algae eating snails and should max out at one per ten gallons.

Nassarius snails and cerith snails spend the majority of their time in the sandbed turning the sand. They come out at night and during feedings. A tank can house a maximum of one per gallon.

What about other crabs?

The most common crabs aside from the hermit are the arrow crab, emerald crab, and sally light-foot. Arrow crabs eat bristle worms day and night. Arrow crabs can be kept in concentrations of one per tank up to 75 gallons and one more for each additional 75 gallons of water. They do fight sometimes.

Emerald crabs are great algae eaters and specialize in removing bubble algae from aquariums. Emerald crabs can be kept in concentrations of one per ten gallons while the food supply lasts. Generally, I don't recommend more than one per 20 gallons.

Sally light-foot crabs are general scavengers and spend their time looking for algae and other waste or debris. Sally light-foot crabs can be kept in concentrations of up to one per 20 gallons. This became one of my favorite crabs to keep in a reef tank. They are extremely fast, great cleaners, and regarded as reef safe.

Things to remember:

Cleanup crews are essential to a healthy reef system. Without scavengers in your reef problems are likely to arise. Hermit crabs are extremely important if you ever lose a piece of livestock, because they will devour it before it has the ability to cause an ammonia spike. This one little act of theirs could save your entire ecosystem.

Snails are important for keeping the algae down on your rockwork and glass. They might not clean off every piece of algae, but they will put a serious dent in what is there.

Crabs - such as - arrow crabs have their own specialty. Some eat bristle worms, some eat bubble algae, and some just scavenge for what was left behind. No matter the specific concentrations you have of invertebrates in your ecosystem, remember they are a vital part of a happy and healthy reef.

Responsible Reef Keeping

It is the responsibility of every hobbyist to practice environmentally friendly reef keeping. Releasing livestock into the wild is a terrible idea. It contaminates the natural ecosystem and introduces invasive species.

Most stores will take in unwanted livestock. If you have trouble finding a store to take your livestock you can give it to a reef club or local hobbyist.

Removing coral from the ocean endangers reefs and our global seafood supply. You can help by purchasing aquacultured livestock, when available. Maricultured is another form of reef friendly livestock.

Saltwater aquariums are fire hazards and usually contain poisonous livestock. Clean salt creep on a regular basis and make sure your electrical devices have a drip loop to avoid electric shock and fire.

Ensure children and people with allergies do not get into the aquarium or chemicals. Most corals are extremely toxic and should be kept from children.

Adopt a Local Store

Running a helpful saltwater aquarium store is quite the challenge. When a store gives you good customer service and helps educate you on the ins and outs of your tank, you should reciprocate by shopping only at that store. This hobby is not as profitable as you might think.

I am not saying you can't go to other stores and check them out, but you should support the store that treats you right. You might not think ten dollars is a lot, but it adds up quick.

Spending all your money in one store will also help balance out your aquarium. The employees will start to learn your tank and will be happy to help you if you run into problems.

When you find a great store, tell people. Great saltwater shops need all the help they can get to grow. If you want them to support you and your tank then support them.

The right local store will hold events, training, and offer maintenance. You should be able to get your water tested and trust the results. If you have a problem they should be your first choice for help. This is also a great way to meet fellow hobbyists.

General Coral Placement

These are just general guidelines to get you started. Every single coral is a little different. Because of this, you will need to watch your corals and move them accordingly.

Soft corals prefer moderate light, but they can survive in a wide range of lighting conditions. I recommend starting them in the lower half of the tank and moving them accordingly.

They like moderate water flow. It is a good idea to give them enough circulation to keep debris from collecting on them. If they don't extend their polyps you should move them to a lower flow area and keep an eye on them.

Large Polyp Stony Coral (LPS) likes moderate to high power lighting. I usually place them in the top half of the aquarium and move them according to polyp extension.

I have had the best results with LPS in slightly turbulent water flow. You don't want to damage the polyps, but waving movement seems to work well. Watch the coral after placement and move if needed.

Small Polyp Stony Coral (SPS) tends to do best in high light and turbulent water flow. There are some SPS corals that like moderate light. Start your SPS in the top 25% of the tank. Move it around from there until you have good coloration and polyp extension.

Paying for Maintenance

If you don't have a lot of time, but have a little extra spending money, you can hire your local store to maintain your aquarium. There are also independent saltwater tank maintenance businesses.

Most of these companies are willing to do pretty much everything, but they charge per service. You will have to decide how much you are willing to spend.

Generally, hobbyists that hire a company to maintain their tank do it for the water change and water testing. These services can include water changes, testing, dosing, feeding, aquascaping, coral placement, equipment replacement, tank installation, leak repairs, livestock introduction or removal, and more.

The only way to get a feel for the cost of this service in your area is to call around. Get an idea of what you would like to have the service do before you call around. This will give you a point of reference for your decision.

Remember, ask for references. You can never be too careful with someone coming into your home. Not to mention, they are going to maintain your investment. Find out what kind of supplies they use. You can't learn about them if you don't ask.

Have fun with it!

Never forget that this is a hobby. You will probably spend more money in the hobby than you can ever get back by selling everything.

Sure, some people make money in this industry, but it is harder to make money in fish and coral than you might think. Costs are extremely high to keep a reef store operating.

Patience is always a virtue when dealing with a saltwater aquarium.

Go out there, have fun, find a store to adopt, and make some friends. Don't get deterred by minor setbacks. Hobbyists that haven't ever had a crash are rare.

By utilizing this book you should be years ahead of the other beginners. This guide should save you anywhere from hundreds to thousands of dollars.

--Zechariah Blanchard

Creativity, Innovation, and Entrepreneurship

Keys to the Future of Human Society

Find it at any major online retailer.

By Zechariah Blanchard

Copyright ©2010 Zechariah Blanchard

Creativity, Innovation, and Entrepreneurship dives into which aspects of business and society bring about the changes we love and need to move forward. Zechariah breaks down and explains creativity, innovation, and entrepreneurship in a way that is easy to understand.

He offers the reader examples and analogies to help better explain how these things play a crucial role in the future of our society.

The author believes that creativity, innovation, and entrepreneurship have played an imperative role in the past, present, and will continue to play an imperative role in the future.

Mr. Blanchard explores many different areas of creativity, innovation, and entrepreneurship. He also goes into detail about how they can be applied to individuals and groups.

<u>Creativity, Innovation, and Entrepreneurship</u> is available in electronic and paperback form on Amazon.com and at other major retailers. Get your copy right now!

Speaking Engagements and Seminar Training

Zechariah Blanchard is available for speaking engagements within the United States.

Mr. Blanchard can speak on any of the topics from this book or his other books.

You can contact him about the details of a speaking engagement via his website:
www.ZechariahBlanchard.com

You can also contact the author on facebook, twitter, linkedin, and by searching for him online.

Send paper correspondence to:

Zechariah Blanchard

PO Box 677413,

Orlando, FL 32867

About the Author

Zechariah Blanchard was the working manager/owner of a saltwater aquarium store in the Orlando, FL area. During the time he worked in the store he regularly helped well over 300 people with their aquarium needs.

At one point he held classes at his store specifically designed to teach his customers how to better care for their aquariums and livestock. He wrote several different information brochures for his customers – helping them to acquire the knowledge to be smart with their money, their livestock, and their safety.

Zechariah is a saltwater enthusiast who believes saltwater aquariums are not hard if you have the basics down. That is the main reason for the writing of this book. Share the knowledge so that others can enjoy the love of the hobby!

Mr. Blanchard is a disruptive Entrepreneur who graduated from the University of Central Florida with a Bachelors of Science in Business Management. Mr. Blanchard enjoys entering markets with room for rapid advancement.

Contact Zechariah at books@ZechariahBlanchard.com

Made in the USA
Columbia, SC
08 March 2020